Wrapped in Folds of Midnight

Karen Richards

Copyright © 2021 Karen Richards

All rights reserved. No part of this publication including the cover image may be reproduced, distributed, or transmitted in any form or by any means, without the prior written permission of the publisher.

Cover Photography: Deni Cupit Photography

Cover Design: Islam Farid

ISBN: 978-0-6489919-1-5

DEDICATION

This book I dedicate to the man who holds my heart.

None of this would be possible without you.

I love you.

Xx

and in memory of Jas

who wanted to see this book become a reality

Rest in Peace, beautiful girl

CONTENTS

Midnight Lullabies	7
Falling Stars	37
Cosmos of Black	71
Untouched Galaxies	99
Cracks of Light	125
A New Day is Born	157

Midnight Lullabies

Wrapped in Folds of Midnight

meet me by the moon
as midnight strikes
and constellations twinkle
like tiny mirror-balls
floating in a cosmos of black
while on blankets of green
we dance, our bare feet twirling
between dreaming marigolds
to a rhythmic cricket's song
and you dip me into Eden's caress
beneath the promise
of a vibrant new moon

I was an artist without a muse
until he bared to me, his soul
and with eyes bereft of colour
holding my fingertips to his heart
he finally allowed me
to paint him back to life

your laughter resembled that of a child
as you tucked dandelions behind my ear
the seeds cascading through my hair
into goosebumps on my skin
my heart, a bounding chorus
contained in a body
frozen by the moment

I will forever remain
moonstruck by memories of you

I did not ask you to love this fragile heart
so full of fluttering arrhythmia's
that even I am not convinced it is built right
nor did I ask you to hold all of its
feeble delicate fragments together
with hands which were made
to serve a higher purpose than I
but if loving me was an accident
which you fell into while my hands
were busy stemming the haemorrhage
of your own tragically, fragile heart
I do not wish to know a purer love

I have spent a lifetime trying to mould love
into the shape of you
even when it felt completely wrong
I tried to love them into shapes
they were never meant to be
then along came you
my most unexpected
dream come true

when I tell you that I love you
promise me, you will hold my words
like lyrics to the tip of your tongue
and sing them back to me
when I am weak enough
to believe

I believed I was not worthy
of a love like yours
but even when I gave you
one million reasons to leave
you showed me one million
and one to stay

my heart was buried
knee deep in these fallen skies
your love unearthed me

when you finally spoke
the words I had waited
so long to hear
I watched your lips move
yet heard nothing
for I had already memorised
the perfect sound
of being loved by you

I believe this empty space
which created its home
beneath my ribs
was always meant for you
it makes sense now
why love repeatedly
fell through the cracks
yet with you it takes
three insignificant words
pressed against my cheek
the tenderness of your lips
to kiss away my tears
and I can breathe again
just long enough
to fall in love with you
all over again

here I am again
daydreaming of you
translating the language
of your lips on mine
those silent whispers
of everything and nothing
lingering against the warmth
of my neck
then I see you smile
and it tells me
you believe
in the impossible too

you are the reason I see rainbows
painted into shadows
where light should never be found
why I hear melodies through deaf ears
swaying in rhythmic silence
and how I found happiness
in places I had never thought to look

his caress reminds me
of the way night skies
embrace the stars
it is no wonder
I am in love with the dark

if there are moments better than this
curled into the warmth of your chest
listening to rain pummel
the outside world into oblivion
as streetlights and even the moon
concede defeat and extinguish themselves
to storm-ridden skies
then let us search for them
while we drown in the deluge
bodies intertwined
lightning striking against skin
until ecstasy is ours
when again we chase breathlessly
moments just like these
with a fire in our eyes
no storm can douse

I long for that familiar winter chill
where 'neath canopies of stars
we would hide like children
waiting to be found
our fingers, tracing wishes
into cosmic skies
bursting with meteor showers
opened palms, filled with the hope
of two hearts, who were yet to realise
they too had fallen
into dreams fulfilled

allow me to hold you
until your heaving chest
finds calm against my skin
the teardrops dancing
upon your lashes, dry
and your trembling body
takes refuge in
the shape of my silhouette
and softens into sleep
allow me to become, home

just as crescent moons
and clusters of minuscule lights
sprinkled across still waters
define the night
I find myself, coming home
to secrets hidden in the light of your eyes
and the curve of your smile
my body, caressed by the night
craves the touch of your heart and hands
to love even the darkness inside of me

between wisps of climbing jasmine
and hot chocolate moustaches
I found forever in your smile

I will leave these forbidden secrets
in torments of scarlet lipstick whispers
against your skin
clandestine memories
and future promises
that with one touch of my lips
enter your bloodstream
as sins of the flesh

you must realise
there is no escaping love now

there is an echo
creeping through
this delicate heart
which sounds a lot
like you

I cherish midnight lullabies
professions of truth
confessed to soft folds
of my flawed skin
rocking us gently
beyond the point of no return
and into dream-filled slumber
where between rhymes
I find safe harbour
for my heart

if there is anything
I will be guilty of
time and time again
it is loving you
just a little too much

whether it is in silence or chaos
the tender words you leave
inscribed upon my heart
are always tiptoeing
through my mind
saving me, from myself

I am so afraid of losing you
while the world sleeps and dreams
terrified that I will open my eyes
one day and you will be gone
I never considered
no, not for a second
that you might just be afraid
of losing me too

if our love must collapse
beneath the weight of these stars
let us write an ending
worth searching for
in the dark

if I could write poetry about you, I would
but not a word has been imagined
to capture the shape of you
on my lips

Falling Skies

her hands are full
of swords and shields
tread gently
with her heart

you built me a treehouse
in the realms of your imagination
where we could never be found
we laced fingers, like lovers
tucked into endless nights
reciting fairy tales by starlight
sailing constellations in origami boats
folded carefully with our hearts
the cosmos erupting with laughter
as you pushed me higher and higher
on a swing held together on strings of stars
until I had surpassed the curvature of the moon
and found myself falling from view
I no longer know your laughter
your voice or your love
but I will always remember
that you built me a treehouse
in the realms of your imagination
where I will always exist
just for you

hold me
like night skies
hold precious
falling stars
until I too
fade to
black

another day dawns
and I knowingly commit treason
making false promises to my heart
that today I let go
not let thoughts of you
seep into the pages of me
or let that smile penetrate my skin
but over and over, day after day
as another sun falls to rest
this chapter, just like every chapter
begins and ends with you

we burn, like moths
whose wings were too fragile
for these flames
our hearts; ablaze

you say I am as beautiful
as stars scattered across night skies
but they are dying too
hanging precariously by a noose
from the curvature of a waning moon
begging for the darkness
to swallow them whole
and eventually it does
for even the brightest stars bow
beneath the weight of a lifetime of wishes
you place upon their smiles

what do I say, when words fall silent from my
lips? when their quiver form syllables
that in no way convey any morsel
of what my heart wants to say

what do I do when the distance
between my heart and yours is so close
yet too far for my empty palms
to catch the broken pieces
I promised to spend a lifetime mending

what can I give when the only person you need
is the one I cannot be when you need me most

I can do nothing but wait
and pray that everything
I have given, every day before today
will be enough to see you
through the darkness until dawn

I tiptoe this invisible line
between want and guilt
blindsided by the fear
of my want for love
causing the sadness
which creeps quietly
from your lips
and the guilt of not wanting
to save you if it means
letting you go

I am constantly being followed
by shadows of our love
around every corner, in every crevice
are pieces of us
in memories and songs
in the way the wind whistles
through the leaves
and in your smile
every time I close my eyes
I seek comfort in star-speckled skies
the one thing that tied us together
like balloons to a piece of string
but even the constellations
have dimmed in mourning
the tiny sliver of moon
trying to disguise itself
as it hangs its head in tragedy
where do I turn now?
when even the loneliest places shun
this shattered heart
when home is where my heart is
but I have not felt it beat
since you said goodbye
the truth is I am every shade of blue
without you

I was born to bend
mould the curvature of my spine
away from your spineless arrows
laced with symphonies of self-gratification
you insist on pressing like a knife's tip
into the innocence of my skin

believe all you want in my fractured reflection
which in your eyes lies frozen
immobilised by fear
try as you might to hide the truth
I was always born to bend

his eyes held reflections
of the woman I was
and who I wanted to be
he raised me, held me
a sparkler in the dark
never allowing me
to wither and die

what will become of me
now that I do not have him
to hold my heart
open to the light
and stop me from being
swallowed by the dark

I remember now how I loved the way
a breeze could carry your name
lay it delicately like a kiss on my skin
now it blows a gale, rattling my bones
sending shivers of regret along my spine
like a sound I am desperate to forget

even as the words fell from my lips
I could not fathom goodbye
knowing I was losing the one
who has kept me alive through it all

it does not feel real
this sense in my soul
of you slipping away
breeze in my palm
where your hand made a home
the deafening melody of goodbye
tangled in a serenade of silence

I am afraid to breathe
because what if I cannot
without you

I lament upon empty mason jars
grasped tightly between shaking hands
where once they were full of light
now an overflowing darkness
ravaging my soul
plucking tears from my eyes

so lost am I
the sun has ceased to exist
and I am merely hanging on
by shallow breaths and fingertips
with little desire
to chase fireflies in the dark

how do I find my way home
as tumultuous seas crash violently
against my chest
the raging undulation of rogue waves
swallowing whole
the only parts of me worth saving
spitting my lifeless carcass
against jagged rocks
omnipotent darkness sucking flesh
from my bones
until I am nought but a ghost
who calls to sailors in the night
begging for a lighthouse
to guide me home

you tied your heart
like a balloon to my wrist
kissed promises
softly to my neck
that no matter how dark
the skies became
I would never become lost
to your heart

now all that remains
is a lifeless piece of string
and a lesson learned
that promises
are made to be broken

I feel my heart unravel
a million tiny threads
and wisps of heartbreak
floating the cosmos
I grasp at them, desperate to
pull them back into my chest
but what good would it do?
I would just return
to the agony of losing you
still here I am, delicately
gathering and sewing
every lost thread of you
back into my dreams
until I can feel the familiar rhythm
of half agony, half hope
lying in wait for the
pleasure and pain of love

I have forgotten how daylight feels
a soft kiss of sunshine on my skin
the caress of a southerly breeze
whispering through my hair
how the perfume of daisies
filled my soul with memories
of carefree yesterdays
in the moments
before darkness descended
and I became accustomed
to being burnt by the sun
torn to shreds by the wind
and reminded that daisies
are nothing but weeds
now I find my solace in nightfall
where all hope
shines lighter in the dark

this body is a vessel for my mayhem
an urn for the ashes
of my scattered thoughts
and shards of a scarred heart
skin and flesh; a flimsy veil
between fake smiles and detonation

I am held hostage to the night
swathed by the unfurling aromas
of petals languishing
from forgotten roses
stems tied with black ribbons
still a sting to their thorns
egyptian cotton, kissing skin
left haunted by the indent
of a ghostly silhouette
and dreams which turn to goosebumps
surrendering delicately upon my skin
but not in the ways we had planned
not in the illusion in which we live
as hostages relinquished to the night

we have been trying to piece together
an impossible puzzle
taken far too long to realise we do not match
the picture on the box
that our edges do not meet
as if someone maliciously ripped
the tabs from every piece
to ensure we remain incomplete
and they succeeded
as we pack our love away
to be placed high on a shelf
and forgotten
with all the broken things
we always meant to fix

the illumination of an amber moon
casts a glow onto this empty bed
where it once kissed your furrowed brow

I cannot fathom
the emptiness I feel without you
this guttural, razorblade
taste of goodbye

so, for now, I will draw the curtains closed
fold my shattered heart into memories
of when you were mine

and will myself to believe
this time, love will conquer all

when I am ravaged with loneliness
I swallow moonbeams whole
in desperate hopes that someone
will be enticed by my glow
and maybe just once the moonlight will stay
long enough to stave off the darkness

I write as if people cannot hear
the reverberating sound of a soul in turmoil
as if they cannot see through the pretty words
of love and hope and see me frozen still
placard in hand reading
'please help me, I'm drowning'
as if my whispers are not being drowned out
by booming voices of people
more worthy of being heard
I am tired of these four walls
with curtains drawn to keep out the light
empty bottles lining counter tops
because I am frantically searching
for the long-awaited numbness they bring
like these words
which I know will remain unread
yet still, I write

today, I watched the last sunflowers die
and wondered if it was all just that simple
one moment our rouged cheeks
are being kissed by the sun
and the next, our breath is stolen
life plucked like diamonds
from the soiled, sodden pockets
of Mother Earth without so much
as a whimper

perhaps we should not call this love
refrain from the guilt of placing
such a beautiful word upon our lips
and letting it fall so vehemently
that even the sky cries with pity
over what we have become
we let ourselves build walls
so impenetrable, so indestructible
that now, not even a crack of light
can find its way through this charade
and maybe that is a good thing
so, neither of us can see
the battle scars we have gifted
to each other's wounded heart

I want the memory of us
to be craved like the rains
held captive by angry clouds
until they spill like tears
onto drought-stricken lands
pooling in puddles, ankle-deep
beneath tired boots
you, dancing to memories of us
and a love which once
was as fierce as a storm
destructive, but beautiful too

do you ever stop to consider
how we are as much in the throes
of death as we are life
that reminders of our existence
come with each passing breath
(inhale...............exhale)
same cannot be said of death
creeping closer with every passing day
silently and without alarm
the secret, a self-realisation
that we are forever chained
to this curse of living and dying
only when we can learn
to thrive despite them both
can true inner peace be ours

I am a firefly without fire
a wild heart, tamed
by this constant fight for survival
subconsciously picking
at these fragile wings
so, I can no longer fly
because here in the safe
dark embrace of the earth
there is nowhere left
to fall

Cosmos of Black

and just like that we come to realise
it is all nothing more than smoke
mirrors and sleight of hand
the only magic which still exists
is in the lies we allow ourselves
to believe

as black clouds
shroud the lustre of the moon
I learn I am afraid of the dark

there are no words left
for the utter emptiness that I feel
so, I will draw the chapter closed
place a bookmark
where true happiness
with you was finally found
and pray that I will return
to pick up where we left off
maybe not in this life
or the next but one day
when I can return
the kind of woman
you dreamed me to be

I live in fear of this nothingness
these big black holes
swarming with nightmares
sucking me in and devouring me whole
the misshapen memories
which dance like shadowed marionettes
behind closed lids
and terrorise my dreams
into treacherous trickery
waging a war against sleep
that I cannot win
when night arrives

I am brittle, splintered by
infinite hairline fractures
running the length of my spine
waiting for one final blow
to shatter me
into a million slivers
of never enough

who knew when we fell
so completely into each other
with hearts entwined
that what was to follow
would be the beginning
of an agonising asphyxiation
one heartbeat at a time

it begins with a smile and a kiss
soliloquy-soaked sentences
dripping from those lips
so perfectly formed
with shapes of lust and love
purging wanton desire
so desperately, so rhythmically
to the quickened pace of my heart
left wanting, under the covers of darkness
in a never-ending realm
of anticipation and unfulfillment
as I draw closed another night
with only memories of you

it is the deafening silence
these gaping holes in my heart
that will never again, be filled
where friends became family
and family became a cure
for this ache within
I wish I had known then
what I know now
how it can all disappear
in the blink of an eye
replaced with the deafening
sound of silence

I am angry
the heaving breath
stinging eyes
pounding heart
kind of angry
but there is no one
to set the savage beast upon
but me

is this how it ends?
two birds trapped
in a cage built for one
clawing at these bars
like life on the outside
is less painful than this
our rebellion against fate
this purgatory of hearts
these deaf ears stubbornly
refusing to hear love
softly chirping within
ignoring revelations
that we are simply meant to be
two birds, content
with being caged by this love

when the pain is so crushing
it defies explanation
loneliness becomes a constant companion
and maybe it is just easier this way
while no one can see the sorrow
spilling from my eyes
I can use what little bravery I have left
to convince them that I am fine

you smile as the dagger
is pushed slowly into my chest
one twist could end the pain
but what fun would that be
when you can watch me suffer
for the rest of my days
in a million ways worse than this

I have fallen out of love with living
but you would never know it
never see the pain which hides beneath
taut skin, all that holds me together
my smile, some automated response
to muscle memory of happier days
because I am tired
and it takes less strength to smile
than to hide the desperation
of a withering soul
who has fallen out of love with life

they will not make movies
about me when I am gone
nor scribe me into pages
passed down through generations
my picture will not adorn galleries
or silhouette be cast in bronze
but I hope they will remember
my laugh and my smile
my strength and how I fought
like a warrior to the end

come to me sweet misery
save me from this loneliness
this morbid life of discontent
and repetitious monotony

blanket me in familiarity
a safety of sad tranquillity
delivered by your warm embrace
where I can find sweet salvation
and leave my soul to rest

these blue skies do not match
the dull grey of weeklong insomnia
gnawing at the whites of my eyes
heavy lids refusing to close
because behind them everything lost awaits
walls bearing down so hard against my skin
I cannot catch a single breath
I daydream of dancing again
burying my toes in white sand
and praying for rain
for the raging storm outside
to just once rival the turbulence within
camouflaging these tears
so, I can stop myself from drowning
in this drought

below the darkest light I am lost
deep within in the silence
between echoes of a lone wolf's howl
and the tears of a midnight moon
lost in the pitch-black loneliness
of night blindness
the very same that led me to you
rendering me dazed
in the silhouette of your smile
my attention; drawn away
as the hatchet swinging
from the open cavity of your chest
waited for me to love you
so, you could feast upon my naive heart
below the darkest of light

you picked the perfect flower
with wilted petals
and a stem already bowing
against an angry wind
and crushed it
beneath your dirty boots

I never really stood a chance
against your annihilation
and it hurts to know
of all the flowers
in all the gardens
who fought so hard
to learn to love their smiles

you chose to obliterate mine

can you feel the betrayal of my tongue
or grind of my teeth as they speak your name
how could you?
the mere thought
of lending my mouth to the sound
causes a sting of acidic bile
to rise in the back of my throat
as I swallow it whole
you were a mistake I will never repeat

if freedom awaits
within champagne sunset cusps
far beyond blue skies

why do I teeter
between dreams and nightmares
with each tiny step

masquerading in this
monochromatic monotony
I am desperate to be
unearthed in living colour
but I will forever remain a rainbow
trapped in a lead pencil
bereft of beauty and
left to compose words
invisible in this world

today, I captured the moon
resting against the bluest of skies
and I wondered if she too, was worried
I might not make it through the night

was our fate already written in the stars
mocking me as I cried beneath night skies
overflowing with the ache of loneliness
knowing, that when I found you
I would love you enough to stay
and watch them steal everything from us
with each breath
a moment at a time

words lay coiled around my heart
squeezing the very last breath from my lungs
lips sewn tightly shut to avoid spilling
the unending pain trapped deep in my soul
onto anyone else

tears no longer exist
just a numbness in my fingers
which want to write, but cannot
because the poet in me no longer exists
perhaps she never did

please lord, show mercy
upon my broken soul
allow this cancerous mourning
to take from me, one final breath
draw your glistening sword
across the scars of my flesh
so, I can no longer feel the misery
of promises laced with silence
let the noose tighten around my throat
for there are no words left unsaid
'cept for unrequited sonnets
which fall on deaf ears
as I plead for a finale of mercy

Untouched Galaxies

today I discovered the scent of you
still lingering on my skin
took comfort in aromas
of bergamot and cedar wood
clinging to the nape of my neck
where you held me one last time

I revisit those moments
of love and happiness
now etched into closed lids
instead of my arms
a better woman born
from being loved by you

you will always find me waiting for you at sunset
with constellations scattered throughout
mousey brown hair and golden beams
reflected in hazel eyes
as the loneliness of moons and stars and I
collide against darkened skies to bring your
dreams to life
in your darkest hours we have felt your tears
and listened to your deepest fears
if only you could lift your eyes just once
you would see that we have been here all along
singing sweet lullabies of sunset song

if I were an artist
I would bring you to life
trace your silhouette onto empty sheets
paint your hand into mine
mould myself against your chest
scrawl 'I love you' onto the tip of your tongue
but I am no artist, nor will I ever be
so, you will remain at most
the unfulfilled romantic notion
of an incompetent heart

Become loves lantern
a star filled **c**onstellation
guarding midnight mo**on**s

I am anchored to this falling star
nursing freshly burned scars
seared with the ferocity of its life
into my impressionable skin
until there is nothing
but a fine dusting
of our charred remains
raining onto the earth
as if we never existed
at all

listen closely to soft whispers
left upon wafts of baby's breath
feel the kiss of moonlit skies
gentle upon your saddened brow
find beauty in the little things
which fill your heart with joy
that is where I left
all your memories of me
kept safe, for you to find

you exhale deeply
eyes, welled with tears
as if this is the moment
you have waited for
the softness of my heart
in the palm of your hands
and safe refuge in the cradle
of my arms

I long to feel the softness of your fingertips
tracing the curvature of my spine
unzipping my skin with a deft touch
removing layer after layer
of scars and impurities
until you find me worthy of your love
I just wonder what will be left of me
when you do

I lay, wrapped in folds of midnight
cacophonous cicadas
serenading their sharp symphonies
in time with the gentle rain
tapping at my window
capturing contrasts
between light and shade
turmoil and the peace
which is finally mine
these moonbeams dancing
softly across your lashes
our swathed silhouette
cast onto walls
which have only ever
witnessed me, collapsing
beneath the weight of silence
now testify to me gracefully falling
for hope

gravity became just a memory
the second your fingers
brushed the hair from my face
smiling lips colliding
into each other's atmosphere
weightless, breathless
ascending through time
colliding into familiar
yet untouched galaxies
filled with meteors and falling stars
merely astronauts
lost in the trembling eclipse
and minuscule space
of this veiled embrace

she is the kind of girl who sways
eyes closed, swathed by moonlight
face, kissed softly by newborn stars
until she too, shines
in that fraction of a second
she is enough, for him, for herself
for this judgemental world
and for the first time
without desire to be anything more
than a girl with a galaxy of promise
in her eyes, who dances
to the song of her moon

his touch feels like
pastel lilac wisteria
creeping across bare skin
soft glow of wanton eyes
sensually ravaging
mind, body and soul
eager to discover
new beginnings in me

I close my eyes, squandering moments
interred in memories of us
losing myself in the sways and rhythms
of eager lips and champagne-flushed skin
where a softly spoken 'I love you'
fills the tight crevices between us
until there is no space left to breathe
and we collapse, trembling
beneath the weight of the stars
coiled together in a single silhouette
under the light of the moon
yearning for encore after encore
to sweet autumn melodies

I want my touch to speak
in a way my words cannot
to leave an outline of sonnets
in the crook of your neck
and quickened rhythm
of iambic pentameters
pulsing in your veins
to hear the glorious sound
of soft, sensual alliteration
creep from your lips
as you lose control
I want to be the only poetry
you will ever know

pacify my soul with fingers
softly strumming supple skin
lips crooning choruses of sighs
halos discarded as heartstrings
lay tangled in a mess
between these sheets
we were always partial
to a case of the blues

I love the way
you sigh my name
with the softest smile
as our lips touch
the beauty of each syllable
pronounced so perfectly
they could birth new stars
into heavenly skies

Wrapped in Folds of Midnight

your fingers trace
every contour of my form
leaving painted stars
scattered between
full moons and half truths
I am euphoria bound
swathed in galaxies of you

to this rhythm I move,
sway of hips; entice his lips
like moth to a flame

your eyes shimmer
in the night light
the creases of yours smile
making them sparkle
like rivers of light
exciting my soul
and making me fall
back into the memory
of the moment we met
and our love became
a replica of us
unexpected and wild

pull me closer, let your fingertips
bring a blush to my cheeks
as I nestle into the crook of your arm
content, absorbed
into the only space in this world
which holds the shape of me

you carry me
as if I am as light as a feather
upon a sombre breeze
like the heaviness of my soul
is not making your back ache
and you do it, always with a smile
with lips which radiate hope
like dandelion wishes
dancing softly on closed lids
and I am intrigued to discover more
of what you find beautiful
in me

hold my hand, as we are birthed
into the unknown
where time is an irrelevant burden
not ours to know
spend our days bathed in sunshine
breeze dancing wistfully upon our skin
not weighed down by regret of a tomorrow
which may never be ours
let us squander these nights
making love by moonlight
as days climax into a firestorm of stars
applauding our strength to live
in this moment with hope of the next
yes, hold my hand and break free with me
from the tightening shackles of time

Cracks of Light

I am always just fingertips
away from happiness
close enough
I can feel its warmth
sighing against my skin
but never close enough
to make it mine

I ache for loneliness
simply because I adore
the way I feel
each time
it is vanquished
by your kiss

when they trace your deepest scars
with a loving caress
kissing each one
with the same tenderness
as the unblemished parts of you
and when they find perfection
where you believed there was none
learn to accept their truth
and make it yours

please do not shatter these fragments of me
so delicately held with your strands of hope
do not let them slip between your fingertips
just to watch them disappear
into the depths of all I have ever known
hold me within your velvety embrace
just a few moments longer
allow me time to catch my breath
then witness my emergence
from this eternal fog
birthed, incandescent into a galaxy of stars
with promises of forever tattooed into my skin
wished back to life, with love

you have stripped me bare
standing here before you
all veils I once hid behind
lay crumpled on the floor
consuming every inch
of my exposed soul
even fully clothed
you invent new ways
to bring me undone

I never wanted to fall in love
I knew I needed time
to heal and grow and find myself
yet here I am, filled with the
familiar rising of butterflies
but this time, I do not feel scared
this time these butterflies
are not made of glass

you ask me
why this time
love feels different
the only answer
I can find
is that your heart
has found sunshine
after a lifetime
of shade

I was caught
in suspended animation
like a falling leaf
somewhere between
life and death
just waiting
for you to breathe
love back into this
lifeless heart

I long to witness flames
dancing in your eyes
the laughter of family
filling full-moon skies
beneath the Milky Way
as you pull me closer
into the warmth of your jacket
cool breeze tousling my hair
soft lips against my cheek
turning to a smile
watching worlds collide
into all your dreams come true

I existed, swathed in blue
until I caught sight
of myself in your eyes
blooming into curves
of alluring light

when the only audible sound
is the echo of your own heartbeat
ricocheting the vast emptiness
do you deeply appreciate
the soothing comfort offered
in the rise and fall of a chest
not your own

I wonder if I will ever reach the point
where I can stare into the mirror
and with all honesty
accept the woman looking back
by then I hope I will have learned to love her
as much if not more, than he does

there is nothing more comforting
than the sweet surrender
of city streets after midnight
the shadows of dim streetlights
kissing places no one ever sees
silhouettes of bending boughs
from token trees planted
to draw our attention from
the monotonous grey
of our dull city hearts
dancing nonchalantly
to and fro
in a rhythm all their own
while we tiptoe the streets
reciting sonnets
to the faceless hoards
of displaced hearts
as the city that never sleeps
suddenly falls silent
but for poetry audible
only after dark

with a smile broader
than sunburnt horizons
I let myself fall in love
with the idea of you
I never dreamt
one day, we would
turn these butterflies
into dreams come true

she is the kind of girl
who still makes daisy-chain crowns
cross-legged in the grass
stitching strands of hope
through open wounds
whiling away hour after hour
practicing her smile
so, one day
when the world finally notices her
there will be no room left for grief
no faded bruises left to find
nothing left of that broken little girl
who survived it all
by adorning her demons
in daisy-chain crowns

do not confine me to a box
built to house my spirit
not while I still draw breath
or press my bones into cedar grain
until the knots become a part of me
I am not yet ready to be
rather let us bury our roots
in the here and now
and learn to grow with grace

do not pen the eulogy with my story unfinished
instead write me poetry
of longing and love
and recite it against my cheek
so, I can know who I am to you
in this moment

do not adorn my casket
in pastel peony shades
which will wither and die in time
plant me a flower
every day of my life
so, I may bask in the beauty
of today

we dance barefoot on asphalt
skin doused by tumbling rain
eyes closed, oblivious to the flicker
of red, amber, green, moving in time
across rainbow waters
we hear nothing but the tempo
of feet sashaying
along these endless white lines
the tremor of passing cars
beating in our chests like cavemen
in tempo with our hearts
until finally, the crash of eager lips
causes a head-on collision
into the car crash that is love

you are allowed to break
to want your weary body
cradled with love
for your cheeks to become
saturated with tears
to feel lost, without purpose
without strength, without hope
but you cannot build a home there
in the middle of those ruins
you are allowed to break
but you cannot give yourself permission
to be broken

I am burying love between these few lines
on pages of a book you will never read,
hundreds of love notes addressed to you
which I will never send
because you believed
love should be spoken, never composed
yet you, you interrupted every word I said
even my pen falls silent
tired of writing in braille for blind eyes
which refuse to feel
maybe one day you will find them
and thumb your way through
these tear-stained words
letting them seep, deep into your soul
by then I will be gone, I already am
my pen frantically scrawling new chapters
for someone who did not hesitate
to read between the lines

I used to feel nothing
in the emptiness
now everywhere
there is you

I am forever reminding myself
that after pummelling squalls
even the sea can soothe itself calm

if our universe
is composed of imperfect beauty
and flaws we are blind to
why then, can we not find
that same wonder in ourselves

drops of rain
skim windowpanes
and I wonder
why they plunge
to their deaths
so eagerly
perhaps I am wrong
and it is simply
a taste of life
they seek

I survived today because of you
because you refused to doubt my strength
defending me with words and swords
opposing the want to wallow
in the shallows of perceived weaknesses
you pulled me to my feet
to defy my own tenacious will
forcing me to revolt against inevitable surrender
even when I dug heels in like an obstinate child
who was hell-bent on raising that white flag
I was lost, afraid and in need of hope
but I survived today, because of you

I am still learning
to love my scars
to see them as triumph
instead of tragedy
and to be grateful
that because of them
I am favoured
the privilege
of yet another day

the moon whispered
'I give back only the light
which I find inside you'
and for a moment; I shone
just a little bit brighter

there is so little time
so few fleeting moments
to immerse yourself in
that you cannot
accept anything less
than someone who loves
one hundred percent
of you

every life is a unique story
with the same ending
make yours one worth
writing about

A New Day is Born

they believed her
lost to a chaotic mind
she simply found home
in elysian fields of gold

I have a gypsy heart
and nomad toes which long
to frolic in blades of green
the sway of trees
fanned by gentle breeze
and fingers which dream
of touching parts of you
no one else can see
places known to only me
your heart, always meant to be
the long-lost home which tames
this lonesome gypsy heart

when I am gone
bury me beneath blankets of autumn
return me to the same earth
which holds death inside its leafy embrace
then revisit me in the throes of spring
caressed by the warmth of the sun
just in time to watch me rise and bloom
once more

it is only when these cracks appear
in my spine, paralysing my body
leaving me broken, unable to go on
that he reminds me
these cracks were put there with purpose
to let the sunshine in

untie my mind from these
tangled strands of deception
relax the noose from my thoughts
so, I might again breathe in
the beauty of a dawning day
and not fear the darkness
that awaits me beyond
blood-orange moons
let me finally break loose
of the chokehold
which skews my reflection
and instead
kiss me with hope
touch me with longing
hold me with love
and remind me
what it is to be free

A New Day is Born

I find sanctuary in chaos
where oceans kiss cheeks of sand
as they gyrate in an endless tempo
only we, who are born of the spray
from raging seas can understand
where churning crescendo's crash
hard into the cliffs of our gypsy souls
in recesses only tempestuous squalls
can tame our wild-child hearts

suddenly the world is ablaze
with unfamiliar colours
so vivid, even my bones
can feel their intensity being absorbed
like paint on a blank canvas
I have been set free
of this monochromatic misery
and born again, into the light

A New Day is Born

there is contentment to be found
in the soft murmur of busy bees
suckling pollen from breasts of spring
tilted stems, reclining against a midday breeze
undulating sun-kissed petals
reaching proudly skyward
which in my most desolate moments
remind me of the value and beauty
in this constant repetition of one last breath

flowers paint themselves
into seasons of Spring
their polychromatic efflorescence
of heaven scent
birds and bees
suckling from nectar's nipple
as pollination of heaven,
earth and wonder
link together; hand to petal to wing
sprouting life from within blooms
of hope and brighter days

A New Day is Born

you are the blazing fire
of a summer sunset
woven into the familiar calm
of fresh lavender sprigs
your tactile fingers coaxing submission
gently, expertly from these lips
the wonder and want of your eyes
turning my inebriation into your delight
as you unzip my skin
allowing the light
to penetrate us both
my soul; your compulsion
your touch; my undoing

I am grounded
but longing to be
as wild as a gypsy
I am silence
and yet the most beautiful sound
that you will ever hear
I am gentle
with the fight of a lioness
I am a plethora of contradictions
but still, who I want to be
I am woman

I am living proof
that amazing things can rise
and thrive from darkness

while you sleep, outlined perfection
rising and falling against the backdrop
of these tiny, dancing cracks of light
I will tuck stars beneath your dreaming lids
bury them into closed palms
so, when loneliness creeps across your skin
and silent midnight prayers kiss your lips
you will be reminded darkness
is only ever conquered
by the rise of the light within

A New Day is Born

it is a moment that even
scribbled lines cannot capture
the rising sun pausing
briefly above our intertwined fingers
as it creeps along
these crumpled sheets
a grazing, golden glow
left languishing across beaded skin
a new day is born and so are we

it was the first time I felt heard
on my knees; before God
with my bleeding heart
in outstretched palms
I prayed for a miracle
and he sent me
you

A New Day is Born

I yearn to discover solace
in the ebb and flow of tides
the majesty of vast cobalt blues
languishing against jagged shores
choir of dolphin hymns
rippling through my body
like a chorus of contentment
my despair, lured from the depths
breaching into an ethereal light
to freedom

I will meet you there
in the pause between
dreams and dawn
where we can no longer decipher
fantasy from reality
and peace is finally ours

A New Day is Born

there was something beautiful
about the way she smiled
the way it swept to the corners of her eyes
causing them to squint and sparkle
with the warmth and glow
of a summer breeze, kissing her face
and she seemed familiar, somehow
like a long-lost friend, returned from battle
taking her first steps toward freedom
and as I wiped a lonely tear, she did too
today, against all odds and endless storms
in the mirror, I found my smile; reborn

on wisps of a gentle wind; hope floats
launched by tender tongues
and poised pens pressed to parchment
alliteration dripping from lips
which long to recite songs of the wild
yet remain tamed in familiar silence
hope floats, amid lanterns of language
stilling the beating hearts of strangers
birthing butterflies from dismal days
and delivering light into the dark
trusting, no matter the distance
we are hearts; intertwined
when hope floats

ABOUT THE AUTHOR

Karen Richards resides in Australia, she is a writer of poetry and prose, author of The Way My Words Fall and contributor to a year long poetry publishing project 'Poetry 365'

Karen has been writing poetry for 30 years and enjoys connecting with her audience with emotion and simplicity through shared experiences.

Karen currently writes to a social media audience and her work can be found on Instagram.

ABOUT THE PHOTOGRAPHER

The spectacular cover image for this book came from the keen eye of Hobart Photographer Deni Cupit.

His eye for detail and entertaining captions make him a favourite in the local photography world.

He has been involved in Karen's #stillandmetaphor project, coupling the amazing photography of Tasmanian Photographers with her poetry.

You can find more of Deni's Photography
Instagram: @deni_cupit
Facebook:
https://www.facebook.com/DeniCupitPhotography

www.ingramcontent.com/pod-product-compliance
Lightning Source LLC
Chambersburg PA
CBHW050313010526
44107CB00055B/2225